Second Grade Is the Best!

by Mrs. Martino's class

with Tony Stead

capstone

Jobs in School

We love being in second grade! Why? Because we have a great teacher who teaches us how to be better readers. We learn how to be great friends to the other students in our class. Our class, school, and neighborhood are full of people who help us every day. And that got us thinking. What kinds of jobs do we see around our school? What would it be like to do these jobs? We did some research to find out.

The Teacher

by Matthew

Teachers have an important job. They help children learn by making learning fun. Let me tell you more about teachers.

Teachers have to study at school for a long time. Our teacher even went to college. They have to know a lot. And they have to know how to teach it all to other people. Teachers also go to meetings. They have to talk to parents and other teachers. They may give extra help to some children. Teachers also make sure that children behave well.

In the evening, teachers mark books and plan lessons. Being a teacher is hard work!

The Principal

by Zachary

Principals get to decide how to run the school! They also have to keep everyone in the school safe.

Let me tell you more about the jobs principals have. Principals have to go to school for a really long time. Principals have to know math, reading, science, and social studies. As principal, they have to talk to lots of people including kids, teachers, and parents. They have to lead meetings and tell people what to do. They need to think of great ideas for lessons and activities.

I would like to be a principal. Then I could run the school!

The School Secretary

by Kennedy

Secretaries help everyone in the school. They answer lots of questions, including from adults. Secretaries need to be friendly and organized. They need to be good at using computers.

Here is a list of things school secretaries do:

- Answer the telephone
- Help teachers, kids, moms, and dads
- Keep lists and records up to date
- Make appointments for parents to see teachers
- Write school newsletters
- Organize the school

Being a secretary is a busy and varied job.

The Librarian

by Riley

The librarian makes sure we have the right books in the library. He or she decides which books to buy. When new books arrive, the librarian lists them on the computer and makes sure they go in the right place. The librarian helps people find books in the library. Librarians have to be really good readers.

Here are some facts about librarians.
- They read a lot of books!
- They like kids!
- They do a lot of research.
- They know how to put away books.

School Nurse

by Trevor

There are two types of nurses—a hospital nurse and a school nurse. A school nurse sometimes works in a hospital, too.

School nurses keep everybody in school safe and well. They have to train hard so they know what to do. When somebody gets hurt or sick, the nurse is always there to help. She keeps kids with allergies safe. She helps children if they get hurt. We can talk to the school nurse if we are worried about anything. She will help us.

The Janitor

by Morgan

A janitor's job is very important. Janitors keep the school clean and safe. The janitor at our school is the best janitor ever! His name is Mr. Paul. He fixes everything, and he builds things inside and outside our school.

Janitors have to know about tools and machines. They may have to use snow blowers or even fix a leaky sink. They check the heating systems to make sure they work. Sometimes, janitors have to work in the evenings when school is closed.

It helps if janitors like children at school. Mr. Paul loves the kids! He laughs every day.

All Working Together

by Victoria

All of these people, and more, help to make second grade the best! So many people come together to help make our class great. Our teacher helps us learn new things. The principal, janitor, and nurse keep us safe. The librarian helps us find great books to read. The secretary helps us find things out. They all work hard to make our learning fun!